Jim
Henson

Inventors and Creators

Jim
Henson

Deanne Durrett

KIDHAVEN PRESS

THOMSON
GALE

Detroit • New York • San Diego • San Francisco
Boston • New Haven, Conn. • Waterville, Maine
London • Munich

Library of Congress Cataloging-in-Publication Data

Durrett, Deanne, 1940–
  Jim Henson / by Deanne Durrett.—[Rev. ed.]
    p. cm. — (Inventors and creators)
  Includes bibliographical references (p.   ) and index.
  Summary: Discusses the life of Jim Henson, creator of the Muppets,
  including his early life and influences, the development of the Muppets
  and their increasing success, his early death, and his legacy.
    ISBN 0-7377-0996-0
    1. Henson, Jim—Juvenile literature. 2. Puppeteers—United States—
  Biography—Juvenile literature. 3. Television producers and directors—
  United States—Biography—Juvenile literature. 4. Muppet show
  (Television program)—Juvenile literature. [1. Henson, Jim. 2. Puppeteers.
  3. Television producers and directors. 4. Sesame Street (Television
  program). 5. Muppet show (Television program).] I. Title. II. Series.
    PN1982.H46 D87   2002
    791.5'3'092—dc21

2001003958

Copyright 2002 by KidHaven Press,
an imprint of The Gale Group
10911 Technology Place, San Diego, California 92127

Contents

Creative Genius and Master Puppeteer

Creative genius and master puppeteer Jim Henson designed a new type of puppet especially for television. He called this unique cross between hand puppets and **marionettes** (puppets with strings) **Muppets**. Practicing long hours before a mirror, Jim developed techniques that gave the Muppets lifelike gestures and facial expressions. As a result, the skill of the **Muppeteer's** hidden hands became the breath of life for characters that captured the hearts of adults and children around the world.

Sesame Street's cast, including Bert and Ernie, helped children learn the things they needed to know. These included the alphabet, how to cross the street, and how to get along with different kinds of people. *The Muppet Show* characters, led by Kermit and Miss Piggy, entertained all ages.

Jim Henson used his Muppets to share his positive outlook on life in a way that he hoped would make the world a better place. He loved his work and enjoyed

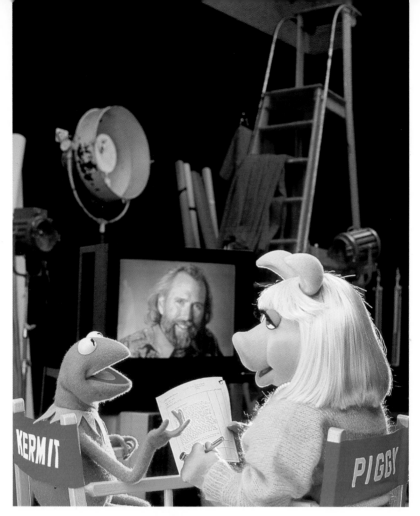

Two of the most beloved Muppets, Kermit the Frog and Miss Piggy, with their creator, Jim Henson, in the background.

every day as it came. He believed that learning should be fun and encouraged everyone to follow their dreams.

Jim Henson did not live long enough to realize all his own dreams. Henson died on May 16, 1990, of a dangerous form of pneumonia. He was fifty-three and expected to have many more productive years. Fortunately, Henson had staffed his company with creative people who shared his outlook on life. As a result, when Henson died, his company lived on to carry out his dreams.

Chapter One

The Young Puppeteer

James Maury Henson was born on September 24, 1936, at King's Daughters Hospital in Greenville, Mississippi. His parents called him Jimmy, but when he grew older, his friends called him Jim. He was the second son born to Elizabeth Marcella (Brown) and Paul Ransom Henson.

Paul Henson worked for the U.S. government as an agricultural scientist. He studied crops that could be grown in Mississippi and used for grazing cattle.

"Mississippi Tom Sawyer"

Jim grew up in Leland, a small town eleven miles from Greenville and the hospital where he was born. A creek runs through Leland and in front of the house where the Hensons lived. Jim, his brother, and their cousins fished from a bridge over the creek in summer. Jim described himself as "a Mississippi Tom Sawyer [who] rarely wore shoes"[1] in summer. In winter, however, the boys sometimes ice-skated on the frozen creek. It was a good place—where Jim and his friends talked and played, and

As a grownup Jim Henson never forgot what it was like to be a boy.

A girl and a boy stroll along a wooded street in Leland, Mississippi, Jim Henson's home town.

where he could have time alone to dream boyhood dreams. Memories from this time would prove to be valuable to him and the Muppets. In fact, Kermit is named after one of Jim's boyhood friends. He named another Muppet after a crop (bird's-foot trefoil) his father studied in Mississippi. He said he honored "that crop in a Muppet named Herbert Birds-foot—a very dry lecturer."[2]

School Days

Jim loved art. In elementary school he added artwork to his reports and projects. Although he said that he was an average student, he made excellent grades.

Jim also loved making people laugh and enjoyed being in school plays. He was not good at team sports and was usually the last one chosen for a team. After school he sometimes played tennis and board games with his brother and friends. He spent most of his free time drawing cartoons or painting. He also enjoyed reading and going to the movies. He loved the Oz books with their strange characters and made-up worlds. *The Wizard of Oz* was the first movie he saw, and when he was grown, he still thought of it as one of his favorites.

A scene from the movie *The Wizard of Oz,* one of Jim Henson's favorite movies.

Before people had television in their homes, they listened to radio programs. Some were music programs. Most, however, were plays and skits performed by actors reading scripts into radio microphones. One of Jim's favorite radio programs was Edgar Bergen and Charlie McCarthy. Edgar Bergen was a ventriloquist and Charlie McCarthy was one of his dummies (a type of hand puppet). Jim knew that Charlie was a dummy and Charlie's voice came from Edgar Bergen. Still, through the magic of radio, Charlie seemed real, and Jim tried to imagine how he would look in real life.

Move to the Washington, D.C., Area

By the time Jim was in fifth grade, his father had finished his research project in Mississippi. The Henson family moved to Hyattsville, Maryland, just outside Washington, D.C. This brought Jim near his grandparents whom he called Dear and Pop. Dear and Jim shared an interest in art, and Jim loved watching her paint with watercolors and oils. She recognized Jim's talent and encouraged him to pursue it.

About two years after the Hensons moved to Hyattsville, modern technology offered Jim a new afterschool pastime. The birth of television offered a new arena for his creativity and artistic skills.

Television Arrives!

When television arrived in the American home about 1950, Jim wanted one in the worst way. He drove his parents crazy until they bought one when he was in seventh or eighth grade. It was love at first sight—Jim loved television. And he loved the puppets that starred in their own shows. One program he especially liked was *Kukla, Fran and Ollie.* The hand puppets, Kukla (a clown) and Ollie (a dragon), were operated by Burr Tillstrom behind

Edgar Bergen and his friend Charlie McCarthy sparked the imagination of young Jim Henson.

the scenes while Fran Allison (the live star) stood beside the **puppet theater** and talked with the puppets. Jim also watched *Life with Snarky Parker.* Deputy sheriff Snarky Parker and his Western pals were marionettes operated by puppeteers Bil and Cora Baird. Marionettes are loosely jointed wooden dolls. Strings connect their movable body parts to a control bar. Puppeteers stand behind the puppet theater and dangle the puppets in front of a curtain or painted set. They twist and turn the control bars to make the puppets perform. They usually act out a play or sing and dance.

Puppets and Art

When Jim entered University Park High School, art still held his interest. He drew cartoons for the school newspaper, made posters for school events, and designed sets for several school plays. Thinking of puppets as another art form—something else he could design—he joined the puppet club. In the puppet club, he also designed scenery for the puppet theaters. Through high school Jim planned a career built around his artistic talent; however, he did not think this career would involve puppets.

First Job

As graduation neared, Jim began looking for a summer job. He heard that WTOP, a local television station, was looking for a puppeteer for a children's show called the *Junior Good Morning Show.* Jim saw this as an opportunity to work in television and applied for the job.

A friend helped Jim build some puppets: Pierre, a French rat, and two cowboys named Longhorn and

Puppeteer Burr Tillstrom (center) poses with his puppets Kukla (left) and Ollie (right).

Shorthorn. Jim described these puppets as "sort of normal hand puppets."[3] He gave them wide mouths that made them unique. Jim got the job and performed his puppets on television three weeks before the show was canceled. He did not have time to be disappointed, however. Producers at another station, NBC affiliate WRC-

Marionettes (pictured) move as the puppeteer pulls their strings.

TV, had seen Jim perform and recognized his talent. They offered him a job on a cartoon show. Jim worked the rest of the summer of 1954 with Pierre, Longhorn, and Shorthorn. By fall he had saved enough money for college tuition, plus the job would provide money for other expenses.

Chapter Two

Kermit and Cookie Monster Team Up

In the fall of 1954, Jim continued working at WRC-TV and enrolled at the University of Maryland. He still planned a career in commercial art and spent much of his spare time painting and drawing. His class schedule, however, pointed in another direction. It included acting, stagecraft, scene design, and puppetry.

Sam and Friends

While Jim studied puppetry during his freshman year, he learned new techniques that improved his television performance. Impressed by the improvement, producers at WRC-TV offered Jim his own show in May 1955.

Sam and Friends was a five-minute spot before *The Tonight Show*. The show consisted of short skits. Many of these skits required two puppets, which meant Jim would need more puppet characters and another puppeteer.

Jim chose Jane Nebel, a young lady in his puppetry class, as the second puppeteer. Jane showed good

A building at the University of Maryland where Jim Henson enrolled in 1954.

craftsmanship in building puppets, plus she had a zany sense of humor that worked well with Jim's. They made a good team, and the show was the beginning of a long relationship.

On *Sam and Friends*, Jim operated one puppet and Jane operated another. Sam was a bald puppet with big eyes and a round nose. He always wore a sport coat and tie. Jim created many strange creatures from his imagination as Sam's friends. None of the puppets spoke while they acted out wild and crazy skits to music. They danced, chased one another, and sometimes one strange creature appeared to eat the other.

The First Kermit

None of Sam's friends were intended to be anything specific. Jim later explained that all the "characters for the local show were abstracts."[4] One was a green lizardlike creature that Jim had made from his mother's old green coat. He cut a Ping-Pong ball in half for the eyes and

Jim created Kermit using an old coat and a Ping-Pong ball.

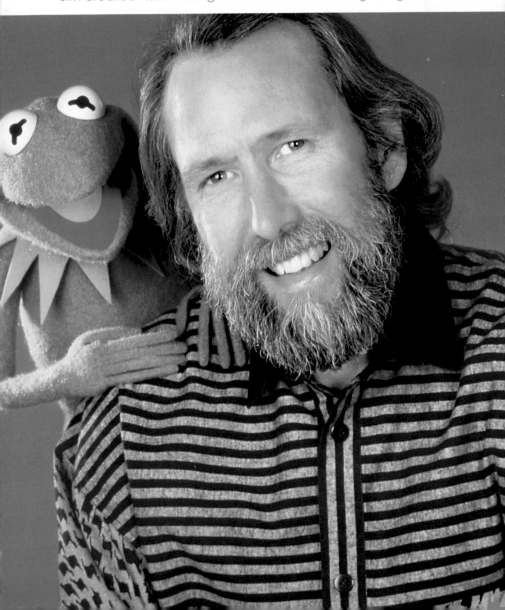

called the new creature Kermit. Jim named this puppet after Kermit Scott, a Leland playmate.

The first Kermit hand puppet was not intended to be a frog. Jim said he was far more lizardlike, but actually he was an abstract, "just a creature."[5] Many of these creatures were the early generations of puppets that would later become the famous Muppets.

Television Techniques

Television brought the audience and the puppet up close and face- to-face. Jim saw the opportunity for a new type of puppet and new puppet techniques. He used the best features of three types of puppets—hand puppets, rod puppets, and marionettes. For example, Kermit is a hand puppet with a soft, flexible face. His arms and legs, however, are operated with stiff wires, like a rod puppet. In the past, however, hand puppets were limited by the size of the puppeteer's hand. Jim wanted to make larger puppets. He also wanted these large puppets to have flexible faces that could be manipulated by the puppeteer's hand. With this in mind, Jim carved the heads from foam rubber and covered them with soft fabric. The large puppets, however, require more than one puppeteer. One puppeteer operates the head while one or two others work the arms and legs. Jim named his creations Muppets because they are a combination of marionettes and puppets.

To use the television close-up to its best advantage, Jim wanted to make the puppet faces more expressive and their body movements more realistic. Having his own television show gave him a chance to try new techniques and see

Cheerful and expressive Muppets surround Jim Henson.

how they worked. Jim and Jane watched the television monitors as they performed. Jim soon learned that the angle of the puppet's head, how it is moved in relation to its body, and where the puppet is looking create the emotion and give the character personality and attitude.

The Set

Television offered another advantage. The audience only saw what the cameraman wanted them to see. This meant that the puppeteer did not have to hide himself completely behind a curtain. He or she just had to stay *off camera*. This freed the Muppets from the puppet stage and gave Henson the opportunity to create a unique Muppet world. He designed scenery in an elevated set with room for the Muppeteers below, out of sight of the cameras. The Muppeteers could be clearly seen in the studio as long as the camera focused on the set.

Wider Recognition

The local viewing audience loved the Muppets. And so did Steve Allen, the first host of the *The Tonight Show*. The Muppets made their first national network appearance on the *The Tonight Show* in 1956. A green lizard in a blond wig (operated by Jim) and an ugly purple monster wearing a happy face (operated by Jane) were a national success. These two puppets later became Kermit the Frog and Cookie Monster.

Muppets, Inc.

Jim earned much more money than most college students. In his last year of college, he decided to form a legal

The hungry Cookie Monster is a favorite character of girls and boys.

partnership with Jane. They called their company Muppets, Inc.

By the time he graduated from college, Jim was a successful performer and businessman. Still, he did not think of puppets as a career and decided to leave Jane in charge of the business, tour Europe, and become an artist. He later explained, "I decided to chuck it all and go off to be a painter."[6] While he was in Europe, however, he developed a great respect for European puppeteers. He realized that puppetry, like theater, "gives us the ability to look at ourselves"[7] in different ways. Jim wanted Americans to enjoy puppetry as much as Europeans did. He decided to make puppetry his career.

Jim and Jane

When Jim came home from Europe, he asked Jane to be his wife. They were married on May 28, 1959. Jane continued to be Jim's business partner and puppeteer. After *Sam and Friends* ended in 1961, the Hensons moved from Washington, D.C., to New York to pursue network appearances for the Muppets. Jane worked full time in the business until the birth of their second child in 1961. She continued to perform some but was never willing to do puppet voices. When the Muppets began to speak, Frank Oz replaced Jane as the hungry monster.

In the years that followed, Jim and Jane welcomed five children into their family: Lisa Marie born in 1960, followed by Cheryl Lee (1961), Brian David (1963), John Paul (1965), and Heather Beth (1970). Jane stayed home to take care of the Henson children while Jim be-

Puppeteers in Europe, like this young French boy, greatly inspired Jim Henson.

came more involved with the expanding Muppet company. Over the years they drifted apart. They legally separated in 1986. Although they no longer lived together as husband and wife, Jim and Jane remained friends.

Chapter Three

The Muppet Company

Jim knew that many talents were needed to create and perform the Muppet characters. Each person Jim invited into the group brought a special talent to the company. Jerry Juhl was a talented writer who wrote the Muppet scripts and later became head writer. Don Sahlin was a talented craftsman and puppet builder. He created the Muppet look that gave each Muppet a unique personality while maintaining the Muppet family resemblance. Frank Oz became a master Muppeteer who worked alongside Jim as Bert, Cookie Monster, Miss Piggy, and others. Over the years Jim and Frank developed a special relationship similar to the relationship between Bert and Ernie. Jim and Frank did not use a script when they performed Bert and Ernie. They simply acted out a situation as they would relate to each other in real life.

Over the years many other people were added to the staff. Jim chose them all for their talent and abilities. They shared his positive outlook on life and his belief that work should be enjoyed. Many of these people spent their entire careers with Jim's company. For example,

Frank Oz is a skilled Muppeteer and was a friend of Jim Henson.

Don Sahlin stayed with the Muppet company from 1963 until he died of a sudden heart attack in 1978.

Creating a Muppet

Jim and the people he chose to join his Muppet company worked hard to take the Muppets a step further and

Each Muppet has a unique and colorful personality.

make them more real. This involved every aspect of Muppet production and performance. First, Jim and two or three of the others put their heads together to come up with an idea for a character. They made a sketch and gave it to the puppet builder. The puppet builder made a puppet, taking great care in placing the eyes so the character would appear to focus. The scriptwriter created skits for the new character. The personality developed further as the character related to other Muppets.

Jim and the other Muppeteers studied the way children expressed themselves. They watched their body language, the tilt of their heads, facial expressions, and the focus of their eyes. Then they practiced their puppets in front of a mirror to capture lifelike movements and facial expressions. During a performance they watched the puppets on television monitors.

Each Muppeteer performed his or her own unique set of puppets. During his career Jim Henson performed twenty-two different puppets, including Kermit and Ernie. Like an actor playing a part, Jim performed each

Kermit sits on Henson's shoulder while Ernie smiles for the camera.

Muppet with its own personality and unique style. Jim explained that it is important to create the illusion "that these characters seem to move and think for themselves." In other words, the Muppets appear to be real. Jim went on to say that it is hard work, "but hard work can be fun."[8]

Sometimes it was hard for the Muppeteers to separate themselves from their Muppet characters. For example, over the years Kermit became so much a part of Jim that when he talked to friends, his hand often moved as though Kermit were involved in the conversation. It was this ability to imagine the Muppets as real that made it possible for the Muppeteers to bring the characters to life for the viewing audience. As a result, the Muppets seemed as real as any other character created by an actor.

The Muppets come to life as anchorpeople while Henson smiles from a television screen in the background.

By the end of the 1960s, the Muppets were well known and attracted a large viewing audience. In addition, professionals in the industry were impressed with Jim's talents.

Children's Television Workshop

In the mid-1960s, Joan Ganz Cooney and the Children's Television Workshop (**CTW**) began researching the best way to use television to teach young children. They found that children relate best to characters like themselves. They decided to create puppet characters with personalities based on real life. They wanted these characters to face the problems children face and express the feelings that children feel. Jon Stone, a producer and scriptwriter for CTW, had seen the Muppets on the *Ed Sullivan Show* and thought Jim Henson would be the perfect puppeteer for the show. An interview with Jim proved that they shared the same belief that television puppets should be totally believable as living beings. As a result, Cooney asked Jim to create a family of Muppets for CTW. In 1969 a cast of mostly new Muppets moved to morning time and the place that would soon be the most familiar street in the world: Sesame Street.

Sesame Street

Sesame Street—a one-hour daily program—required a large cast. Kermit, Rowlf, and a few suitable old characters joined the cast immediately. Many of the Muppet characters, however, were created especially for *Sesame Street*. These include Bert and Ernie, Big Bird, Cookie Monster, the Count, Oscar the Grouch, and many others.

Big Bird and Elmo welcome Joan Ganz Cooney to *Sesame Street*.

On *Sesame Street* the Muppets did slapstick clowning, acted out skits, and introduced live guests, films, and cartoons. The slapstick brought laughter and at the same time helped teach young viewers to count and say the alphabet. Jim said that "learning should be exciting and fun. That's what we're out to do"[9] on *Sesame Street*. In addition, many of the skits involved the Muppets facing problems young children face today. For example, bedtime is a big event in a preschooler's life. Bert and Ernie skits often involve bedtime and numerous things that keep one or the other of them from falling asleep.

The Muppets won the hearts of children from all backgrounds, and *Sesame Street* was an overnight success. It began as a tool to teach counting and the alphabet. The lovable Muppets, however, established a bond with

Bert and Ernie entertain children at a New York hospital.

young viewers, and before long the show was able to address difficult subjects such as birth and death. When Maria (a human member of the cast) became pregnant, Big Bird shared Maria's experience with the wonder of a child expecting a sibling. Along with Big Bird, children everywhere waited for "the baby to push" its way into the world.

The Muppets soon became welcomed guests in homes across America, where an estimated 6 million preschoolers between the ages of three and five watched the show daily. This number represented only a fraction of the show's total viewing audience—older children and adults were also fascinated by the Muppets.

Sesame Street won the prestigious George Foster Peabody Award for Meritorious Service in Broadcasting in 1970. From that time on, Jim Henson and the Muppets received numerous awards for their performances on *Sesame Street*.

Chapter Four

And Beyond

Jim Henson insisted that puppets were for everyone (adults as well as children) and deserved a spot in **prime-time** television. He held that the Muppets "transcend all age groups . . . [and] delight all ages."[10] The success of *Sesame Street*, however, seemed to cement the Muppets into children's programming. Still, Jim Henson continued to follow his dream. Refusing to give up, he kept pursuing a prime-time Muppet show that would entertain the whole family.

Television Specials

In the early 1970s, the Muppets did several television specials with big-name stars including Julie Andrews, Tom Jones, Goldie Hawn, Dick Cavett, Herb Alpert, Perry Como, and Cher. These hour-long shows aired in prime time, and most of the viewers were adults. Still, the major **networks** in the United States (NBC, ABC, and CBS) did not see the Muppets as adult entertainment fit for a weekly prime-time spot.

The Muppet television specials attracted the attention of a wealthy British businessman, Lord Lew Grade. He

Actress Julie Andrews appears on television with Miss Piggy, one of the Muppets' many guest stars.

thought the Muppets were suitable for the thirty-minute time slot before prime time. This time slot is controlled by **local stations.** Jim negotiated a deal with Lord Grade in 1975. As a result, Henson Associates and Lord Grade joined forces to produce *The Muppet Show.* Lord Grade made a commitment to broadcast a full season (twenty-four episodes) of *The Muppet Show* in England. They also produced a **pilot** to promote the show to local stations in the United States aimed at that 7:30–8:00 time slot.

The Muppet Show

While many characters were created for *The Muppet Show*, Kermit was the star from the beginning. Miss Piggy, however, soon stepped into the costar position. Jim said that Miss Piggy was singing in a chorus of barnyard animals, and when she sang her solo, she "stepped out of the chorus and became a star."[11] This Kermit and Miss Piggy duo, performed by Jim Henson and Frank Oz, stole the hearts of the viewers.

The Muppet Show success began in England and spread to the United States and then around the world. By the end of the third season, more than 235 million

Muppet Treasure Island is one of several successful *Muppet Show* movies.

viewers watched the show in more than a hundred countries. From there it was a short journey to Hollywood, where *The Muppet Show* cast made many successful movies. Jim began experimenting with new puppet forms and made several movies completely unrelated to the Muppets. These included *Dark Crystal* and *Labyrinth*.

The Muppet Show fulfilled Jim's dream of puppet entertainment enjoyed by all ages. Some consider *The Muppet Show* Jim Henson's shining hour. *Sesame Street*, however, is his legacy—the lasting mark he left on the world.

Rainbows and Butterflies

Jim Henson developed flu symptoms early in May 1990. Jim, however, was not much for going to the doctor and chose to let his body fight the infection. As it turned out, Jim had pneumonia caused by a virulent (stronger and more dangerous) strain of streptococcal bacteria. His body was unable to fight this form of the bacteria that usually causes strep throat. By the time he was so ill that he went to the hospital, it was too late for antibiotics to save him. Jim died on May 16, 1990. And the world mourned the loss.

Those who knew Jim best and loved him most celebrated his life at a memorial service on May 21, 1990. More than five thousand mourners fulfilled Jim's request that no one wear black as they crowded into the Cathedral Church of St. John the Divine in New York City. Over the weekend, Muppet workshop personnel had made two thousand brightly colored foam butterfly rod puppets. During the service, mourners waved the butterflies as a tribute to Jim's outlook on life. Muppeteers performed the Muppets as a farewell to Jim.

The Muppets Go On

Some people think that Jim Henson knew he would die young. He had chosen and trained all of the people in the Muppet company to do their jobs well. As a result, the company could go on without him, and they could carry on his commitment to make the world a better place. Jim had even selected and trained Steve Whitmire to perform Kermit. In fact, the whole Muppet cast, except one, would continue performing. Jim's son Brian would take

Jim Henson's son Brian and Miss Piggy answer questions at a New York press conference.

command of Jim Henson Productions. *Sesame Street* would continue. The Muppets would make more movies, and new and different creatures would join the puppet crew.

Frank Oz said he could not perform Bert to anyone else's Ernie. The Bert and Ernie characters became lifeless dolls stored in their drawers. Still, Bert and Ernie will continue to entertain and teach children for generations to come as *Sesame Street* replays twenty years of Bert and Ernie episodes on tape.

Jim Henson's Legacy

Jim Henson not only made the world a better place; his work will continue for years to come. Muppeteers trained by Jim Henson will pull the Muppets from their drawers

Jim Henson continues to inspire people of all ages and backgrounds.

and bring them to life in front of television cameras. Learning on *Sesame Street* will be fun. A multitude of creatures will spread goodwill, teach the golden rule in a nonreligious setting, and help children understand what life is about. People everywhere will have fond memories of *Sesame Street* and be thankful for what they learned there. Adults will join children in waiting to see the next new imaginary world populated by a cast of new creatures produced by Jim Henson Productions but inspired by the memory of that gentle genius Jim Henson.

Notes

Chapter 1: The Young Puppeteer

1. Quoted in Don Freeman, "Muppets on His Hands," *Saturday Evening Post,* November 1979, p. 52.
2. Quoted in John Culhane, "The Magical Madcap Muppets," *Reader's Digest,* September 1997.
3. Quoted in Carol A. Emmons, "Jim Henson and the People Behind the Muppet Mania," *School Library Journal,* September 1984, p. 27.

Chapter 2: Kermit and Cookie Monster Team Up

4. Quoted in Emmons, "Jim Henson and the People Behind the Muppet Mania," p. 27.
5. Stephanie St. Pierre, *The Story of Jim Henson, Creator of the Muppets.* New York: Dell, 1991, p. 35.
6. Quoted in Geraldine Woods, *Jim Henson: From Puppets to Muppets.* Minneapolis: Dillon Press, 1987, p. 20.
7. Anne Commire, ed. *Something About the Author,* Vol. 43. Detroit: Gale, 1986, p. 124.

Chapter 3: The Muppet Company

8. Quoted in John Culhane, "Unforgettable Jim Henson," *Reader's Digest,* November 1990, p. 126.
9. Quoted in Robert Higgins, "The Muppet Family and How It Grew," *TV Guide,* May 16, 1970, p. 35.

Chapter 4: And Beyond

10. Quoted in John Culhane, "The Muppets in Movieland," *New York Times Magazine,* June 10, 1979, p. 60.
11. Quoted in Emmons, "Jim Henson and the People Behind the Muppet Mania," p. 30.

Glossary

CTW: Children's Television Workshop, the creators of *Sesame Street*.

local stations: Television stations that broadcast to a limited area. They produce local news and broadcast a selection of entertainment programs plus network programming.

marionette: A puppet with strings attached to loosely jointed arms and legs and sometimes lips and eyelids. A puppeteer performs this puppet by moving a control bar attached to the strings.

Muppeteer: Puppeteers Jim Henson and his company trained to perform the Muppets.

Muppets: Jim Henson's unique puppet creations; a combination of puppets and marionettes.

networks: Large television broadcasting companies that feed their programming to local stations, creating a system for airing programs nationwide.

pilot: A television special that introduces or promotes a new series such as *The Muppet Show*.

prime time: The most popular television viewing time each day from 8:00 P.M. to 11:00 P.M. (Prime time is slipped back an hour in the Central and Mountain time zones.)

puppet theater: A small stage that conceals the puppeteer and provides a stage for his or her puppets.

For Further Exploration

Books

Stephanie St. Pierre, *The Story of Jim Henson, Creator of the Muppets*. New York: Dell, 1991. A juvenile biography of Jim Henson. The author was a childhood friend of Lisa Henson and knew the Henson family personally.

Geraldine Woods, *Jim Henson: From Puppets to Muppets*. Minneapolis: Dillon Press, 1987. A juvenile biography of Jim Henson.

Websites

Henson.com. www.henson.com The official website of Jim Henson Productions is filled with information about Jim Henson and the Muppets plus links to related and interesting pages.

The Muppets Home Page. http://vr.ncsa.uiuc.edu/BS/Muppets//muppets.html. An unofficial Muppets page filled with links to fascinating information, including how to prepare for a job with Jim Henson Productions and an application for a nonpaying internship.

Index

Picture Credits

About the Author

Deanne Durrett has been writing nonfiction books for kids since 1993. She writes on a variety of subjects but her favorites are biographies. She loves research. To her it is an adventure filled with discovery. She and her husband, Dan, live in Arizona with Einstein (a mini schnauzer) and Willie (an Abyssinian cat). In her spare time, Ms. Durrett likes to play Nintendo and shop for Beanie Babies with her grandchildren.